LEGENDS AND FOLKLORE HAMPSHIRE

BRADWELL
BOOKS

Published by Bradwell Books

Unit 1 (Atlantic), Carrwood Road, Chesterfield S41 9QB
Email:info@bradwellbooks.co.uk

British Library Cataloguing in Publication Data: a catalogue record for this book is available from the British Library.

1st Edition

ISBN: 9781910551509

Design by: Andrew Caffrey

Typesetting by: Jenks Design

Photograph Credits: iStock and credited individually

Print: CPI Group (UK) Ltd, Croydon CR0 4YY

CONTENTS

There are many strange tales told about the New Forest and once upon a
time it was thought to be a stronghold of witches.
iStock

INTRODUCTION

The folklore and folk tales of the British Isles make for an endlessly fascinating study. A glorious confusion of ancient beliefs has evolved over the millennia thanks to the many different races that have settled here. In England they have included Stone Age and Bronze Age tribes, the Iron Age Celts, Romans, Angles, Saxons, Norsemen and Normans.

Into this cultural melting pot have been thrown any number of superstitions and half-remembered tales of cultural heroes, some real, some mythical, and many a mixture of both.

Our ancestors lived very different lives to those we enjoy today. Most were tied to the land and had an intimate relationship with the seasons and the natural world. Few had travelled further than their nearest market town, while many had never even strayed that far from the rustic landscape they knew so well.

Nevertheless, their seemingly limited existence was coloured with an awareness of another world, one where supernatural beings lived alongside them just out of sight; where illness or death could be brought about not by microbes but by witchcraft; and where heroes and villains from a past age lived again in dramatic legends told down the generations.

In this book you will be introduced to just a taster of the legends and folklore which enlivened the days and nights of Hampshire folk a century or more ago. In its pages you will encounter dragons, giants, ghosts, sorcerers and saints, heroic knights and kings. You will learn strange superstitions about the wildlife of the county, about the weather and about good and bad omens. You will also be introduced to some of the archaic customs formerly carried out to mark the seasons of the year and the crucial stages in life.

The folklore of Hampshire paints the county as a wonderfully magical place. I hope you enjoy this brief tour through its wonders.

The Needles are among the Isle of Wight's more distinctive landmarks. The Devil was said to sit on these pillars of chalk and hurl lumps of rock at the mainland. *iStock*

KINGS AND SAINTS

In the Anglo-Saxon period Winchester was the capital of the kingdom of Wessex and, in the 11th century, arguably the royal capital of England. Adding to the city's status was a long-held belief that even longer ago the legendary King Arthur had held his court at Winchester. The Normans were keen to exploit this belief because the stories of Arthur told of him fighting the Saxons, the people whom they had just conquered.

The most impressive reminder of the King Arthur tradition is undoubtedly the Round Table which hangs in Winchester's medieval Great Hall. A number of sources from the Middle Ages state that Arthur had constructed a round table in Camelot so that none of his knights would sit lower or higher in rank than any other. Arthur's Round Table was considered an icon of the chivalric ideal.

The Great Hall Round Table dates from the 13th century, is beautifully constructed of solid oak and is 18 feet (6m) across. It weighs about a ton. It's believed to have been made for King Edward I when he held a tournament at Winchester in 1290. At that time it had legs and would have been used in the usual way. The decoration probably came later; certainly the Tudor rose painted in its centre post-dates Edward I. When the Emperor Charles V visited England in 1552, Henry VIII displayed the Winchester Round Table, claiming it to be Arthur's original. All in all it is a splendid demonstration of how important the King Arthur myth was to the medieval mind.

King Arthur's Round Table hangs in Winchester's Great Hall, an impressive medieval monument to the legendary king. *iStock*

In Harewood Forest, south-east of Andover, can be found a monument called Deadman's Plack. It was set up in the 19th century on the spot where the climax to a romantic legend was believed to have been played out. The adventure took place during the reign of King Edgar when Saxon Winchester was at its height. Edgar is said to have been more than partial to the fairer sex and when he heard of the beauty of the Earl of Devonshire's daughter, he sent Ethelwold, his Hampshire ealdorman, to find out the truth of the reports. If she was as lovely as he had been told, Edgar intended bringing the maiden to his court and making her his mistress.

Elfrida – for that was her name – was indeed a decidedly beautiful young woman, and could also be very charming. So attractive was she that Ethelwold fell for her himself. He sent a misleading report to the king, playing down Elfrida's charms, and then married her. For obvious reasons, he kept the wedding a secret. In time, however, Edgar learned that Ethelwold had taken a bride and invited them both to court. Ethelwold begged Elfrida to disguise herself, to make herself appear ugly, but on the day she was presented to the king, she did the opposite; she appeared in all her radiant beauty fully intending to fascinate her sovereign.

King Edgar was indeed fascinated and it didn't take long for him to discover that she was the much-discussed daughter of the Earl of Devonshire. He was furious at having been lied to by his ealdorman but he kept his counsel so as not to embarrass his assembled guests. He was determined to be revenged on Ethelwold for the deception, however, and the next day organised a hunt in Harewood Forest. The king lured his victim into a quiet part of the forest and promptly impaled him with his hunting spear. Deadman's Plack is claimed to mark the place where Ethelwold fell.

The Anglo-Saxon King Edgar is said to have revenged himself on a deceitful nobleman in Harewood Forest. *iStock*

In the New Forest can be found another monument erected on the supposed site of an untimely death, but this time of a king rather than the victim of a king. William the Conqueror had the New Forest cleared to make it a royal hunting ground. According to legend, one man whose home was taken from him cursed the Conqueror, stating that his sons would die in the new preserve. To an extent the prediction came true. While hunting in the New Forest, his son Richard was gored to death by a stag and several years later his son William, who had succeeded his father as king, was killed by an arrow (the eldest son, Robert, had stayed behind in Normandy after the Conquest). Richard's demise seems to have been a genuine accident, the sort of thing that might befall anyone taking part in brutal blood sports, but the death of William II has long been regarded as suspicious.

King William II ruled England from 1087 to 1100. He was known as 'William Rufus' because of his red hair. On 2 August 1100, William Rufus took part in a hunt in the New Forest with his youngest brother Henry and a group of nobles, including Sir Walter Tyrell. We only have Tyrell's testimony as to what happened on that fateful day. He claimed to have caught a glimpse of a stag running through the trees and instinctively let fly with an arrow. It was a poor shot. The arrow glanced off the animal's side and was deflected into a thicket. Tyrell went to retrieve his arrow and pushed his way through the undergrowth. Then he made a startling and horrifying discovery. Lying on its back he found the body of his king – and it had an arrow embedded in its chest.

Tyrell stared down at the corpse numb with shock, until the sounds of the approach of Prince Henry's hunting party brought him back to his senses. Terrified of being blamed for King William's death, Tyrell fled the scene, eventually making his way to France. After he had found time to reflect on the tragedy, however, he realised that he couldn't have been responsible for the king's death. The arrow which had glanced off the stag's side wouldn't have had sufficient force to pierce his body. Another puzzle was that the king was supposed to be accompanied at all times by a huntsman, a sort of bodyguard, but this man had been noticeably absent. What the worried knight did not know is that this huntsman had come forward shortly after the discovery of William's body and had put the blame for his death on Tyrell. He claimed he had seen Tyrell deliberately aim and shoot the fatal arrow.

The truth about William II's death in the New Forest has ever afterwards remained an intriguing historical mystery. Did Tyrell lie about the accident or was the huntsman lying to cover up his own fatal mistake? Or was it murder, a pre-arranged assassination made on the orders of the young Prince Henry? Henry was crowned king with almost indecent haste, apparently taking advantage of the fact that his elder brother Robert was away fighting in the Crusades. In more recent years, a more abstruse theory was put forward that William's death was a kind of human sacrifice, the culmination of an ancient pagan custom in which unworthy kings are ritually killed off.

The monument called the Rufus Stone now stands where William II's body was found. The area around it is said to be haunted by the ghost of the king, who is unable to rest until the truth of his fate is revealed. The apparition of Sir Walter Tyrell also haunts the New Forest, riding frantically but silently down Tyrell's Lane, the route he took to escape the scene of William's death.

The Rufus Stone stands where King William II met his mysterious end in the New Forest.

In addition to yarns about long-dead kings, there are a number of traditions in the county about its holy men. St Swithun (or St Swithin) is the saint most closely associated with Hampshire. He was Bishop of Winchester in the 9th century. St Swithun is best remembered today for a popular saying regarding the great British summer:

> St Swithun's Day, if thou dost rain,
> For forty days it will remain;
> St Swithun's Day, if thou be fair,
> For forty days 'twill rain nae mair.

St Swithun's Day is 15 July. The reason for this superstition appears to be linked to the bishop's burial. A 12th-century chronicler, William of Malmesbury, states that just before his death, Bishop Swithun refused the honour of being buried within the cathedral but instead opted for a humbler place outside, where people coming to worship would tread on it. The spot was near the west door, and rainwater tended to run down the eaves and drip on his grave, providing an early link between Swithun and rainfall.

Swithun's damp and humble grave attracted many worshippers, so on 15 July 871, according to one version of the tale, the monks of Winchester decided to disinter his body in order to give it a high-status burial place within the cathedral. At once a terrific rainstorm blew up, showing the holy man's displeasure at having his bones disturbed, and the monks took the hint and abandoned the project. Another version says the incident took place on 15 July 971, but that the monks persevered. It is certain that at about this time St Swithun's remains were deposited in a shrine dedicated to him within the cathedral. This shrine was destroyed in the Reformation. (Further weather lore will be found in the 'Superstitions' chapter.)

Swithun was canonised because of the number of miraculous cures that were believed to result from praying at his grave and later at his shrine. As his choice of burial place shows, the future saint was a humble man. As bishop, he restored and had built a number of churches. Part of his job was to dedicate or rededicate these churches, but he would do so without pomp or ceremony, walking to them alone and at night to avoid drawing attention to himself. One of Swithun's acts of generosity was to order the construction of a stone bridge over the River Itchen on the eastern side of Winchester, at a spot where poor people from the surrounding countryside were in the habit of wading across to get to market.

An old story tells of a typically kind and modest miracle performed by Swithun at this bridge. One day an elderly woman was crossing

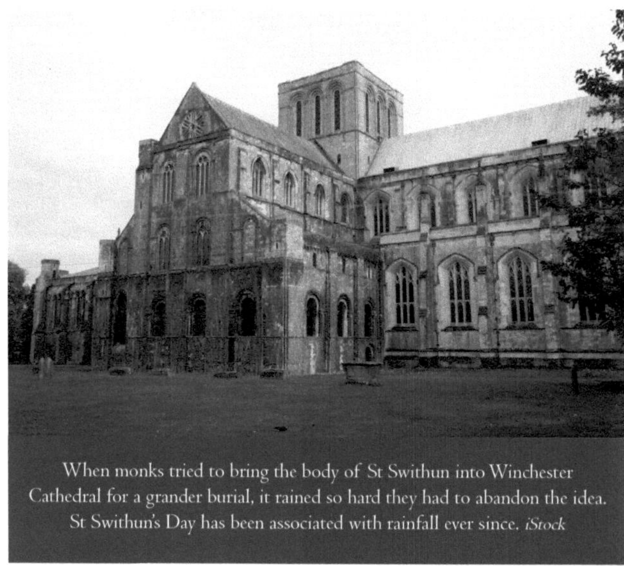

When monks tried to bring the body of St Swithun into Winchester Cathedral for a grander burial, it rained so hard they had to abandon the idea. St Swithun's Day has been associated with rainfall ever since. *iStock*

over it laden with a basket of eggs which she was hoping to sell. Unfortunately, she dropped them and they smashed on the cobbles. The bishop was passing and saw the accident, which was something in the nature of a minor tragedy for the poverty-stricken woman. Swithun spoke soothing words to her and the eggs miraculously repaired themselves and were made whole. This miracle is recorded in one of the stained glass windows in Winchester Cathedral.

As well as miraculous cures, St Swithun's presence was made known in other ways long after his earthly death. In the 11th century, Emma, widow of King Cnut and mother of Edward the Confessor, found herself charged by her son of 'lechery' with the then Bishop of Winchester, Aelfwine. The queen and the bishop had a close relationship but no romance. Nevertheless, it was decided that to prove her innocence this unfortunate woman would have to undergo a trial by ordeal. She was to walk over nine red-hot ploughshares laid out in the nave of the cathedral. If she was innocent, God would preserve her. If not...

The night before her ordeal, St Swithun appeared to Emma. The saintly ghost told her he would be with her and to have no fear. 'Daughter,' he said, 'be steadfast to undergo your fate.'

The following day Emma watched as the ploughshares were heated up and laid out before her. She turned her face to heaven and, praying to St Swithun, she stepped lightly across the glowing metal. She suffered no injury and her feet were unscathed. As her innocence was proven beyond doubt, surely some faces in the cathedral must have turned as red as the ploughshares, including King Edward's. In gratitude for her deliverance, Queen Emma gave up one of her manors to the church for each one of the ploughshares; Bishop Aelfwine also donated nine manors; and the embarrassed king donated three.

Contrasting with these legends about the saintly Swithun is a yarn about a later Bishop of Winchester. This bishop – he is unnamed – asked the king of the time to grant him a parcel of land belonging to the royal hunting ground of the New Forest. The king was annoyed by the request from the worldly bishop but smilingly agreed. He said he would donate as much land as the bishop could crawl around in a day – an area that was likely to be tiny, for the clergyman was grotesquely overweight. His belly protruded so far that His Majesty thought it unlikely his arms would even be able to reach he ground.

The bishop proved equal to this challenge, however. He had a cart made to take the weight of his enormous stomach. Lying face down in it, he was able to propel himself around more than four miles of rough country. As he did so, his weight threw up a bank of soil. This bank is still to be seen today and is called the Bishop's Dyke.

One of the many picturesque churches dedicated to St Swithun in Hampshire. This one is at Headbourne Worthy. *iStock*

HEROES AND MONSTERS

Hampshire's folk stories tell of a time when fearsome creatures haunted the countryside, monsters that could only be killed by the bravest and most resourceful members of the community.

The Bisterne dragon is one of the best known of these legendary beasts. It features in the coat of arms of the Berkeley family who at one time owned Bisterne Manor, a Tudor house near Ringwood. The earliest version of the story of the dragon claims that it was dispatched by an ancestor of the Berkeleys after feeding on cows and people and 'spoiling' a number of prior would-be heroes who had tackled it. The account of the dragon appeared on a document believed to date back to the early 17th century which used to be kept at the manor house:

'Sir Moris Barkley the sonne of Sir John Barkley, of Beverston, beinge a man of great strength and courage, in his tyme there was bred in Hampshire neare Bisterne a devouring Dragon, who doing much mischief upon men and cattell and could not be destroyed but spoiled many in attempting it, making his den unto a Beacon. This Sir Moris Barkley armed himself and encountered with it and at length overcame and killed it but died himself soon after. This is the common saying even to this day in those parts of Hampshire, and the better to approve the same his children and posterity even to this day do beare for their Creast a Dragon standing before a burning beacon.'

A later version of the story, noted down by Wendy Boase in her excellent book on *The Folklore of Hampshire and the Isle of Wight*, published in 1976, adds some details. Sir Maurice Berkeley, she writes, covered his armour in sticky bird-lime and attached to it shards of broken glass to further protect himself from the dragon's claws and teeth. This added protection wasn't quite enough, for although Sir Maurice succeeded in slaying the monster, he did so at the cost of his own life. He had taken with him his hunting dogs, who threw themselves valiantly into the fray, but they were killed by their adversary's fiery breath. The place where the adventure took place was afterwards known as Dragon Fields. At one time statues representing Sir Maurice's hounds stood on a terrace at Bisterne Manor.

A third variant of the legend of the Bisterne Dragon appears in a 1925 book by Douglas Goldring, called *Nooks and Corners in Sussex and Hampshire*. Mr Goldring states that the knight who killed the dragon was called Sir Macdonie rather than Sir Moris and, according to him, Sir Macdonie's deed was rather a lame one, quite unlike the fierce fight described above. He crept up to the monster's lair and placed a jug of milk outside it. Then he hid himself in a glass case (which seems a strange thing to do) until the dragon sniffed out the bait. While it was contentedly lapping up the milk, Sir Macdonie sneaked out of his oddly transparent hiding place and stabbed the dragon with his sword.

Considered even more dangerous than a dragon was the cockatrice. These creatures were reptilian in appearance but had a head and feet like those of a cockerel. They were believed to spring from eggs laid by a cock — an unlucky event in itself (see the 'Superstitions' chapter) — and then hatched out by a snake or a toad. Although the cockatrice was much smaller than a dragon and might seem a rather

St George is the patron saint of England but Hampshire also had its dragon-slaying heroes. *iStock*

silly-looking critter, it was deadly. It was extremely venomous and one glare from its eyes was enough to kill.

A cockatrice was said to have been hatched by a toad in the cellar of Wherwell Priory. This building dates only from the 19th century, which would suggest that the events must have occurred in comparatively recent times. Perhaps this would explain why the owners were unaware of the horrific nature of the creature, for when it was small they fed and looked after it: a medieval family would never have made such an error. As it grew, the cockatrice became more and more savage, and hungrier and hungrier. Soon there came a time when the beast was only satisfied with human flesh. It broke out of the cellar and went on a rampage around Wherwell.

The local authorities offered a reward of four acres of land to anyone who could rid the neighbourhood of the monster. The challenge was met by a clever servant employed at Wherwell Priory by the name of Green. He knew that when it got tired the cockatrice returned to its old home, the vault below the house where he worked. He got hold of a sheet of steel which he polished until it became highly reflective. Then he lowered it into the cockatrice's lair while it slept. When it awoke, the first thing the monster saw was its own reflection. Mistaking it for a rival cockatrice that had invaded its nest, it threw itself on the mirror in a fury. The steel withstood the assault and the stupid creature continued to fight its own reflection for hours on end, until it became exhausted. Then the cunning Mr Green sneaked in and swiftly slew the oblivious cockatrice with a spear.

Four acres of land cleared in Harwood Forest and bearing the name Green's Acres used to be pointed out as proof of this tall tale. For many years the tower of Wherwell Church was ornamented with a splendid weathervane in the shape of the cockatrice. In the 1920s this was taken down and is now on display in Andover Museum. There certainly seems to be some evidence that the legend pre-dates the building of Wherwell Priory and it may be that the story's action was switched to this prominent house many years after it was first related.

A cockatrice, taken from an old heraldic device. It might look a bit silly, but the cockatrice was a deadly creature which once caused havoc around Wherwell. *iStock*

Another monstrous beast once made life a misery for the good people of Highclere. It had its nest in a yew tree near the church and was called a 'grampus'. It's odd it had this name because 'grampus' was generally used to identify any one of a number of large aquatic animals in the days when natural history was much less advanced than it is today. Dolphins, killer whales and basking sharks might all have been labelled a grampus at one time. Whatever it was, the Highclere grampus was dealt with not by a brave knight but by a parson. He exorcised it with bell, book and candle, suggesting that the creature was more supernatural than natural. It's possible that the story, which has only survived as a fragment, may always have been intended as a joke.

Alongside dragons and their kin, the monsters which most commonly feature in British folklore are giants. The Old Testament makes several references to races of gigantic peoples, and this made it all the easier for people to believe that certain ancient monuments and prominent features in the landscape had been created by giants. For example, prehistoric burial mounds on Breamore Down and south of the Andyke both bear the name Giant's Grave.

Silchester, in the north of the county, is arguably England's most important Roman site and certainly the one that has been most extensively excavated. Calleva Atrebatum is the original Latin name of the town buried under the fields at Silchester. According to a local tradition, the town was formerly inhabited by a giant rejoicing in the prosaic name of Onion. In the days before the archaeologists took an interest, Roman coins occasionally picked up in the fields by the local people were given the name 'Onion's pennies'.

A Roman milestone which stands on a common a mile further north was said to have been thrown from Silchester by Onion. The imaginative have interpreted weathering on the stone as the marks of Onion's massive fingers. Because it is known as the Impstone, an alternative story grew up that it was the Devil who hurled the stone, but the name appears to be a contraction of *imperator*, the Latin name for a Roman commander.

As an aside, I might mention those features in the Hampshire landscape for which the Devil was supposedly responsible. The Roman road between Silchester and London was called the Devil's Highway; there are two Devil's Ditches and two Devil's Punchbowls

There are many stories of giants from around the British Isles, including Hampshire. This one was drawn by the incomparable Arthur Rackham.

in the county; three burial mounds near West Tisted are called the Devil's Jumps; the Devil's Dancing Ground can be found on the Downs above Southampton; and a copse near Selborne was once known, no one knows why, as the Devil's Pleasure. Each of the two Devil's Ditches are also known as Grim's Ditch, but this is an alternative name for the Saxon god Woden, who was also held responsible for creating ancient earthworks throughout southern England.

Other giants to have formerly plagued Hampshire include Angoulaffre. He was fought and defeated by the popular hero Roland, supposedly at the place now called Rowland's Castle. Another hero who appears in a number of English folk tales is Guy of Warwick. In Hampshire he is credited with killing a giant called Colbrand, who belonged to a company of Danes who were laying siege to Winchester. The death of Colbrand brought about the end of the siege and the rest of the Danes were routed. The fight between Guy and Colbrand is said to have taken place on a field near Winchester called Danesmead.

Ascapart was the name of a giant who legend states caused mayhem around Southampton at about the time of the medieval Crusades. His days were numbered, however, when a knight named Sir Bevis arrived in the port. Sir Bevis was a carefree individual, an expert swordsman, brave but full of the knightly virtues of chivalry. He had seen a fair bit of the world, wandering wherever adventure led him. He suffered a spell of imprisonment by the Saracens in the Holy Land but even then his luck held out, for a beautiful local girl called Josiane fell in love with him and helped him to escape. Sir Bevis made his way back to England, finally arriving in Southampton.

As soon as he learned of the presence of the marauding giant, Sir Bevis determined to seek him out. He encountered Ascapart on the Downs and immediately challenged him to a fight. The conflict between them was a long and terrible one but brave Sir Bevis was the eventual victor. The slain giant was buried under a vast earthen mound called Bevis' Mount. The Mount was probably originally a prehistoric barrow but it has long since been ploughed away. However, the name still exists as that of a hamlet near Southampton.

The oddly named Blackgang Chine is a ravine in the cliffs on the Isle of Wight. Its picturesque qualities made it one of the island's early resorts, as Victorians pondered over its yellow cliffs and the red-stained stream which ran between them. Today its wild beauty has been somewhat disguised by the addition of an amusement park. Something in the yellow soil kept Blackgang Chine largely free of vegetation but, according to the story which was once attached to the place, it was at one time covered in shrubs and flowers and was delightful to look upon. Unfortunately, it was also the home of a cannibalistic giant who lived in a cave in the Chine. His name was Chale and he had the nasty habit of snatching children and then roasting them alive for his dinner.

This sort of thing couldn't go on for ever, so a holy man bravely took it upon himself to rid the Chine of its horrible resident. He entered Chale's dark and forbidding cave and found the giant surrounded by tiny skeletons and all manner of loathsome creatures, including toads and serpents. The holy man placed a curse on the giant and on the place where he had carried out his ghastly deeds. According to a book called *Tales and Legends of the Isle of Wight*, written as long ago as 1839 by Abraham Elder, the curse also blighted the place where he lived:

Nor flowers nor fruit this earth shall bear,
But all shall be dark and waste and bare!
Nor shall the ground give footing dry
To beasts that walk or birds that fly;
But a poisonous stream shall run to the sea,
Bitter to taste and bloody to see!
And the earth it shall crumble and crumble away,
And crumble on till Judgement Day.

This, says Mr Elder, is the explanation as to why Blackgang Chine ended up presenting such a bleak appearance.

Monsters of an unspecified sort were formerly said to haunt an old gravel pit near the village of Tadley, and they were held responsible for the occasional unsolved disappearances of unfortunate people.

An old postcard showing the ravine at Blackgang Chine, the former home of a giant who liked to feed on children.

The gravel pit was one of the places claimed as the location of a mythical Treacle Mine at Tadley. Treacle, clearly, cannot be mined and this fabulous idea belongs to the wishful thinking of the nursery. It bears some relation to the 'Big Rock Candy Mountain' of the well-known American folk song. Nevertheless, the idea of the Treacle Mine lingered long in the lore of the village and a number of theories have been put forward to explain the legend.

One oblique suggestion was that 'treacle' referred to a treacle tin containing a hoard of gold coins dating from the reign of George III. This was supposedly dug up many years ago by a small boy in a garden in Back Lane, a place which ever afterwards was jokingly called the Treacle Mine. More prosaic is the theory that the Treacle Mine was a dump of treacly-looking oil left behind by American airmen during the Second World War. This sounds like a modern attempt to explain the name on rational grounds. A big and rather smelly pig farm outside the village was also given the name, but doubtless as a joke. The fact is no one knows the origin of the Treacle Mine myth, nor where it was supposed to be situated.

The final story in this chapter features a human monster or, if you prefer, an anti-hero. It is a tale with which you will already be very familiar but you may be surprised to find set in the Isle of Wight. In the 14th century there was a harbour town called Francheville. It was razed to the ground by French invaders in 1377 – Newtown was later developed in its place. Tradition states that the French met no resistance in the town, and this is why.

A few years before, Francheville had become overrun by a plague of rats. They were everywhere and got into everything. They ate all the stored grain and then moved on to the food in people's kitchens. They even drank the wine and beer. Eventually they began to attack and bite small children. The townsfolk had done their best to rid themselves of the plague. Ratcatchers had been employed but had failed. Cats had been brought to the town from all over the island but the savage rats proved more than a match for them. Carcasses baited with poison and left around the streets attracted the vermin but also brought disease.

A £500 reward was offered by the mayor to anyone who could rid them of the rats. In response a mysterious individual arrived to offer his services – the Pied Piper. The Pied Piper began to make his way through Francheville, dancing and playing sweet trills of music. The rats responded. Indeed they were entranced by the piping. They emerged from the sewers and the cellars and began to follow the Pied Piper by the thousands, forming a living, writhing carpet. He led them down Silver Street and Gold Street until they reached the harbour. Then, still playing, the piper got into a boat and punted it out into the sea. The rats followed and were drowned.

Francheville was now free of every rat and the Pied Piper returned in triumph to claim his reward. The ungrateful townsfolk refused to give him his money, however, and the mayor ordered him out of the town. The furious piper did as he was bid, but he did so playing his pipe. This time all the children of the town followed him, entranced like the rats had been. He led them into the woods and neither they nor the Pied Piper were ever seen again. The townsfolk became so demoralised after the loss of their children that Francheville fell into decay and no one had the will to resist the French invaders when they stormed the town.

The legend (minus the French invasion aspect) is world famous, but not as a tale belonging to the Isle of Wight. Its true home is, of course, Hamelin in Germany. The fable of the Pied Piper of

Hamelin appeared in English in a book published as long ago as 1605 and by that time was already of some antiquity. The Francheville–Newtown version appeared in Abraham Elder's *Tales and Legends of the Isle of Wight* in 1839 but in no prior local histories. Folklorists believe that Mr Elder may simply have borrowed the legend as a means to explain the demise of Newtown, which had become a hamlet by the author's time.

The Pied Piper of Hamelin had his counterpart on the Isle of Wight, if a Victorian collector of folk tales is to be believed. *iStock*

THE FEAR OF WITCHCRAFT

For many centuries it was believed that misfortune, illness and even death could be willed upon a person by another skilled in mystic arts or who had been given the power to do so by the Devil. Because witchcraft appears in the Bible (for example, in the story of the Witch of Endor and the conjuring up of a demon for King Solomon), the 'dark arts' were believed in as firmly by educated people as the illiterate.

It might seem the height of foolish ignorance to believe in witchcraft but it should be remembered that, prior to the 18th century, almost nothing was understood about the causes of disease. Microbes were unknown. We believe in the virus giving us a cold even though we have never seen it and our ancestors believed in the existence of witchcraft with the same degree of certainty.

So firm was the belief in witchcraft that someone accused of cursing an animal or human to fall ill or die was treated just the same as if they had poisoned or murdered their victims by more orthodox means. The criminal justice system saw no difference: the end result was all that mattered. By the dawn of the 17th century, however, Europe had fallen into the grip of a 'witch mania', fuelled in part by the resurgence of bubonic plague and by religious insecurity fanned by the Renaissance. No one was safe from being accused of being a witch. Lonely old women, especially those who had previously been known to provide herbal remedies, harmless love charms and the like, were early targets but even the nobility found themselves accused, often by the unscrupulous as a means of getting them out of the way. Thousands of supposed witches and male sorcerers were hanged or burned alive as the mania swept across Europe.

Hampshire seems to have escaped the worst of this grim business, and indeed I have found only one stray reference to a witch trial in the county, that of a 'Widow' Walker in 1579. Nevertheless, belief in witchcraft remained strong in Hampshire. In common with folk tales from all over the country, the Hampshire witches were believed to be able to turn into hares. The reason for the link between witches and hares is unknown, but it may reflect a cult association in the time of the Celts. When the warrior queen Boudicca was

The witches' sabbat. Images like these helped fuel the fear of witchcraft in past centuries. *iStock*

beginning her uprising against the Romans in AD 60/61, she released a hare and the way it ran determined her plan of attack.

Kate Hunt was one such witch. Legend has it she lived in Curdridge in the 18th century and had the ability to turn herself into a giant white hare. A gargoyle on the church tower is supposed to represent her. Kate was greatly feared and she was thought to have considerable magical gifts. When some men felling trees near Kate's cottage allowed some large branches to fall into her garden, they were astonished to find the next morning that all the trees they had felled, including the offending limbs, had somehow been moved into the road, where they blocked the traffic. The tree fellers wasted a day having to move the timber back again.

Kate's reign of terror came to an end when a man loaded his shotgun with slivers of silver snipped off a number of coins. He went out hunting for the white hare while she was scampering across the fields and he managed to fire off a fatal shot. The wounded hare struggled back to the cottage and there Kate became human again before expiring.

At Breamore there was another witch who enjoyed taking the form of a hare. She liked to spoil the fun of huntsmen by leading on the hounds and then changing herself back into a woman just as they were about to pounce on her. An unusual homely detail is that this witch had grandchildren. On one occasion, when she was scampering about, she became careless and was very nearly caught by the hounds.

'Run, Granny, run, or the dogs will have 'ee!' cried her grandchildren, who had been watching the sport from her kitchen window. Their unorthodox grandmother had to use her magic to avoid the hounds, by zooming through the keyhole in her front door. She perched herself on top of the stove, kicking her heels as the angry dogs snapped up at her.

This amusing story was collected by members of Liphook Women's Institute in the 1930s and is repeated in *The Lore of the Land*, a splendid volume of English folklore collected by Jennifer Westwood and Jacqueline Simpson. The WI also preserved tales about another witch from their home village. This character could turn herself into a white hare like Kate Hunt, but she wasn't as fortunate as her counterpart from Breamore for she ended up being badly mauled by one of the village dogs. Although the witch immediately

Many witches were said to be able to turn into hares and for this reason these charming animals were often regarded with suspicion. *iStock*

returned to human form, her neighbours noticed she was limping and investigation soon revealed the bite marks on her hip and thigh.

Because of their connection with witchcraft, hares were treated with suspicion by some country people in the past. Many would avoid crossing a hare's path. In addition to turning into hares, some Hampshire witches were also believed to be able to turn into foxes.

Witches could be avoided by crossing over running water, by drawing a cross in the dirt or by throwing down a broomstick in front of them. This would force them to turn back. In Hampshire the bay tree was thought to have protective powers against witchcraft and many people grew them in their cottage gardens.

So-called 'witch bottles' were also employed to ward off black magic or to break a spell. These were usually stone bottles or flasks filled with a variety of substances, including bodily fluids, and then buried round the entrances into a house. If a person was thought to be affected by a curse, the bottle might contain his or her urine, nail clippings and a few hairs. The bottle was then placed on the fire, the heat of which would cause agonies to the witch, until she took off the spell. Sometimes the bottle would burst in the flames, and this too would break the spell.

The Liphook witch was defeated in this way. She was strongly suspected of using her dark arts to make a little boy disabled. His legs became so weak that he could not stand on them and had to shuffle about the floor on his bottom. The witch took considerable delight in visiting this unhappy child, offering fake sympathy and petting him in a way that left him terrified. At length his parents created a witch bottle and put it on the fire. As soon as it got hot, they could hear the witch crying with pain outside their home. She beat on the doors and windows – all of which they had carefully locked – in an attempt to get in and prevent the procedure, but soon the spell was broken. The little boy almost immediately regained the use of his legs.

The New Forest was credited as being the stronghold of the county's witches. As late as the 1930s and 40s there were stories of a coven of witches here, practising ancient pagan traditions. Gerald Gardner, one of the founders of the modern pagan religion called Wicca, claimed to have been initiated into its mysteries by a coven of New Forest witches. Gardner famously stated that he and the other members of the coven tried to use witchcraft to defeat Hitler during the Second World War. He said that in August 1940 they gathered in the New Forest and attempted to create a magical 'Cone of Power' to prevent the Nazis from invading Britain.

A witch bottle – used to break a malevolent spell – explodes in the fire.

THE MISTLETOE BOUGH

As you will see in the 'Journey through Life' chapter, it was formerly the custom for a bride on her wedding day to hide from the groom's friends, whose job it was to take her to church, as if unwillingly, blushing with maidenly modesty. According to an old English folk tale, the result of one of these escapades ended in tragedy. It's possible that a genuine incident inspired the yarn but, like today's 'urban myths', ended up being told about a number of different places. Hampshire, however, may well be the original setting, for not one but two manor houses lay claim to it: Marwell Hall, at Owslebury, and Bramshill House, at Eversley.

According to the legend, many centuries ago, a young woman on her wedding day played hide and seek in the time-honoured manner but chose an unfortunate place to conceal herself. In a seldom-visited attic she found a big, old, oak chest and climbed inside it. Alas, the chest was fitted with a spring lock and the heavy lid slammed shut, trapping the bride-to-be inside. She struggled and struggled to free herself, to no avail, and her cries for help were too muffled to be heard. Her frantic family, the groom and the groom's friends searched all through the house but no one found the chest. The girl's disappearance remained a mystery for many, many years. Then, one day, the attic room was cleared out and somebody forced open the lid of the oak chest to see what it contained. Imagine their horror on discovering a skeleton, still wearing the tattered remnants of a bridal gown!

The Georgian poet Thomas Haynes Bayly popularised the legend in his poem, 'The Mistletoe Bough'. In Bayly's poem, the wedding had taken place over the Christmas season and the bride was hiding from her husband for the fun of it. When it is discovered, her corpse is seen to still be clutching a sprig of mistletoe, given to her by her husband. The tale has been known as 'The Mistletoe Bough' ever since, although in folklore circles its tragic theme is sometimes referred to as that of 'the skeleton bride'.

Bramshill House is a magnificent, brick-built Jacobean mansion, one of the finest in the country. For decades it was used as a training

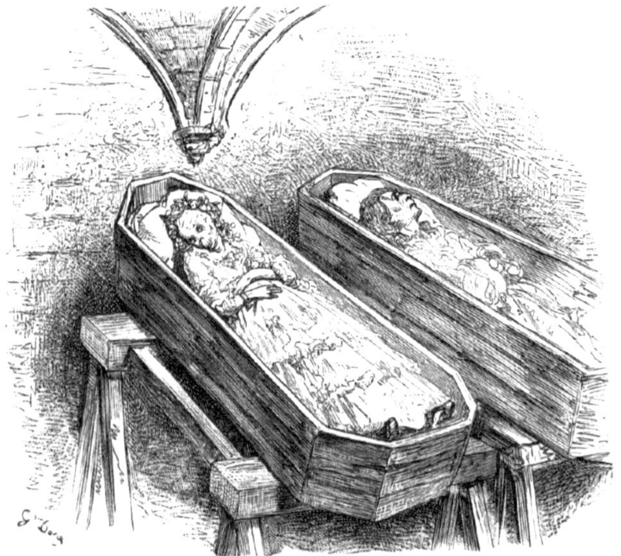

The story of 'The Mistletoe Bough' ends in tragedy for a young bride.

college for police officers but in 2014 was sold to a heritage development company. An elaborately carved coffer in Bramshill's entrance hall is said to be the one in which the skeleton bride was found, and it is known as the 'Mistletoe Bough Chest'. Evidence of the truth of this assertion is said to be the presence of the tragic girl's ghost – the White Lady – who supposedly patrols the house and garden on moonlit nights, still wearing her wedding gown.

Several other ghosts are believed to haunt Bramshill House (one source claims as many as fourteen). In addition to the White Lady there is a Grey Lady, who has been seen in the house but often forlornly lingers around a pond in the grounds, where she may have drowned herself after an unhappy love affair. This sad and rather charming apparition is always accompanied by the scent of lilies. Presumably recalling another suicide is the shadowy figure seen hurling itself from a balustrade. Two female phantoms haunt respectively a bedroom and the Chapel Drawing Room. The latter is dressed in the fashions of the reign of Queen Anne, the former in the styles of Charles I. The Chapel Drawing Room is also haunted by a knight in armour.

The strangest ghost of Bramshill House is the one dressed entirely in green. He is the shade of an eccentric member of the family who owned Bramshill for centuries, the Copes. This gentleman was obsessed with the colour green. As well as wearing exclusively green garments, he painted his rooms and furniture the same colour and would only dine on green fruit and vegetables. It seems certain he suffered from some sort of mental illness, which culminated, tragically, in 1806 when he jumped off a cliff and drowned in the sea.

There are further spooks in the grounds of Bramshill House. The Keeper's Oak – a handsome old tree – is haunted by a gamekeeper of the 17th century who was killed when a clumsy archbishop mistook him for a deer while out hunting and launched an arrow at him. In addition, a mysterious figure has been seen on the old bridge over the river.

Marwell Hall, the other local claimant of the story of 'The Mistletoe Bough', is a handsome manor house dating back to the 14th century. It too is haunted by a female figure in white, presumed to be the ghost of the bride. Some say that the wedding guests have also been seen at Marwell Hall, running silently through the rooms in a ghostly echo of their fruitless search.

Another legend attached to Marwell is that King Henry VIII married Jane Seymour here while his current wife, Anne Boleyn, was being executed on trumped-up charges of adultery. Although Jane was able to give Henry his longed-for heir, she died soon after

The remarkably haunted Bramshill House, sketched by Charles Harper for his 1930 book *Mansions of Old Romance*. iStock

childbirth. Her ghost has been claimed for the house in addition to the 'Mistletoe Bride'. So too has that of Anne Boleyn. Her phantom has been seen striding down an avenue of yew trees in the garden, a resentful expression on her face.

MORE EERIE STORIES

Gathered round the firelight after dark in houses and inns before the days of electricity or even gas lighting, it was natural for people to tell tales of the supernatural. Hampshire boasts many creepy tales (see *Ghost Stories of Hampshire and the Isle of Wight*, also published by Bradwell Books, for lots more).

A tragic tale is told about the village of Vernham Dean in the Test Valley. In the 17th century bubonic plague came to the village, as it spread throughout England. In an attempt to contain the disease, the rector convinced those who had contracted it to isolate themselves in a camp on Haydown Hill. For the good of the community the sufferers agreed, and the rector promised to bring them regular supplies of food and drink. But the clergyman proved to be a coward. He feared that if he went near the camp he would become infected by the plague.

For days the rector dithered over his responsibility and ultimately decided to break his promise and let the people die. Day after day, the plague sufferers vainly looked out for him, but the rector never came. One by one, they all died, either of the disease or from weakness brought on by hunger. Ever since, it is said, the ghost of the wretched rector has been doomed to climb Haydown Hill, making the journey over and over again that he failed to make in life.

Remorse is often given as a reason for a troubled spirit haunting the living. More common is sudden and violent death. At one time

Hampshire's best-known haunted house was Itchel (or Itchells) Manor, at Crondall. The house was demolished in the 1950s but prior to that it was plagued with eerie knocks and thumps which would grow louder and louder through the night. The phenomenon was experienced by a number of credible witnesses. The noises were traditionally supposed to be made by the restless sprit of a former owner, Squire Bathurst, whose despotic, miserly ways had eventually led to his put-upon Italian servant going mad and walling him up alive. The thumps were said to be echoes of those made by the squire trying to free himself or attract attention.

The greed of a man known as 'Miser' Chickett also led to a violent end. Chickett was a successful brushmaker in Upham in the 16th century. He lived in what is now the Brushmakers' Arms, hoarding his money, ignorant of the danger he was putting himself in with

For centuries people have enjoyed telling ghost stories after dark. The audience's interest was bound to be heightened if the tale had a local setting. *iStock*

his miserly ways. It was inevitable that the lure of all that gold would prove a temptation to criminals and one night his home was broken into by a gang of thieves. They brutally murdered 'Miser' Chickett and ransacked the house until they found his hoard of coins. Ever after, it was said, Chickett's ghost haunted the room where he died.

The ghost of Wolverton Manor at Shorwell, on the Isle of Wight, was also a victim of murder. He was a wandering minstrel who had entertained the household and had been lavishly rewarded for his music. He was found a bed for the night. The servants, however, decided to help themselves to the minstrel's fee and they crept up on him in the middle of the night and killed him. The next day they pretended that the minstrel had gone his way at first light, so the murder wasn't at first discovered. However, the presence of their victim's restless spirit, constantly pacing the corridors and bedrooms, soon exposed their cruel deed.

The brutal years of the Civil War left an indelible stain on English history and many traditional ghost stories have their origin in the violence and emotional trauma of those turbulent times. Basing House, near Basingstoke, for example, suffered a devastating siege during the conflict. When it was built for the First Marquess of Winchester, William Paulet, Basing House was the grandest house in Hampshire. It was a palace, five storeys high, and boasted a total of 380 rooms. Today, however, little of it remains standing. The Fifth Marquess, who owned Basing House during the Civil War, was a committed Royalist, and this made it a target for the Parliamentarians. On two occasions the Roundheads laid siege to the mansion without success. Finally, in August 1645, a new siege was implemented, this time with a considerable force of arms under the command of Oliver Cromwell himself. Basing House was eventually stormed and the Fifth Marquess was imprisoned in the Tower of London.

During the siege Basing House was largely destroyed by fire. Afterwards Cromwell ordered that what remained was to be torn down and the bricks and fine stonework sold off. This is the reason so little survives of it today. Nevertheless it is an attractive spot to visit. The ruins are in the heart of an old motte and bailey fortification. Excavations have revealed more of the house than was previously visible and interpretive signs have been set up.

Ghosts of the Royalist defenders of Basing House are said to still linger around the site. One of them is particularly noticeable, for

Basing House as it appeared before its destruction during the English Civil War.

he is remarkably tall. Intriguingly, one of the excavations in the grounds uncovered a number of burials, including one which contained a skeleton well over six feet tall. Perhaps it belonged to the man whose ghost has since been seen.

The author Sir Shane Leslie claimed to have encountered the ghost of King Charles I at Billingham Manor, Chillerton, on the Isle of Wight, when he rented it with his wife in 1928. The apparition was particularly ghastly because all that was seen of the king was his severed head.

At the end of the war, Charles had been imprisoned in Carisbrooke Castle. The Leslies' estate agent told them there was an old legend that on one occasion the king had succeeded in escaping from the castle and that he had made his way to Billingham Manor. He hid in a tiny, coffin-like compartment hidden behind a panel in the drawing room, but became so claustrophobic that he gave himself up. The Leslies claimed to have found a recess like the one described in this otherwise unlikely tale. They also said that at night the house was plagued with the sounds of heavy boots clumping up and down the stairs and the clashing of swords. On one particularly disturbed night, Sir Shane gathered the entire household in the drawing room and they all saw a weird, phosphorescent glow emanating from the place where the compartment was concealed.

Sir Shane boldly slid open the panel and was confronted with the spectre of a floating head staring out of the niche. Its pointed beard and long flowing hair were distinctively those of Charles I. Lady Leslie and other members of the household saw the gruesome apparition before it vanished back into the gloom. Sir Leslie later learned that the ghost would only manifest at Billingham Manor when an execution was taking place, as if in ghostly sympathy. It

The wall surrounding what little now remains of Basing House, whose grounds are said to be haunted by its Royalist defenders. *iStock*

transpired that an execution had taken place at Newport Prison on the day the floating head was seen.

The Monmouth Rebellion was another turbulent period in the 17th century which inspired a number of Hampshire ghost stories. James, the First Duke of Monmouth, an illegitimate son of Charles II, raised a force in the West of England to try to claim the throne in place of his uncle, James II. Monmouth hoped the fact that he was a Protestant would find favour with those who disapproved of the Catholicism of James II. But the rebellion was quashed at the Battle of Sedgemoor and the ruthless 'Hanging' Judge Jeffreys was put in charge of prosecuting surviving rebels.

In 1685, Dame Alice Lisle of Moyles Court, near Ringwood, found herself caught up in the Monmouth Rebellion when she took pity on two men fleeing from the Battle of Sedgemoor and gave them shelter. Unfortunately, the two refugees were caught while in Dame Alice's house. Even though she had no sympathy with the Rebellion, she was charged and found guilty of treason. She was taken to Winchester and executed on a scaffold outside the Eclipse Inn.

Dame Alice's indomitable spirit did not rest easy in her grave after this injustice. Her ghost is said to haunt the Eclipse Inn and her former home (Moyles Court is now a private school). Sometimes she appears appropriately headless.

Another relic of this time was thought to haunt a house in Lymington. This unhappy shade would pace the upper floors at night, opening and closing doors and sighing in despair. The story given to explain his presence is that he was entrusted by the Duke of Monmouth to carry important documents to sympathisers in Holland, together with some valuable jewels to help pay for mercenaries or supplies. The soldier found a smuggler in Lymington who was prepared to take him over to the Netherlands as soon as the tide turned in the morning. He agreed to stay overnight in the smuggler's home, but the daughter of the house got a glimpse of the jewels and convinced her father to murder him for them.

Centuries later, a guest in the house had a vivid dream in which the murdered man showed her the place where the important documents were hidden. It made such an impression on her that she convinced the owners to dig in the spot in the garden indicated in the dream. Soon a slab of stone was discovered under the soil. It was lifted up to reveal a stone-lined hole – but they were disappointed to find that it was empty. Nevertheless, the discovery seemed to be enough to put the troubled spirit at rest, for it disturbed the house no more.

The bitter period of conflict during which Parliament strove to take away the throne from Charles I has been the origin of many English ghost stories. The king himself was said to haunt Billingham Manor. *iStock*

Occasionally a work of fiction can become so established in people's minds that it becomes part of the local folklore. This is the case of the story of Edward Estur, a knight who joined the Crusades in 1364. His effigy is to be found in St Olave's Church, Gatcombe, on the Isle of Wight. Edward took with him as far as Cyprus his bride-to-be, the beautiful Lucy Lightfoot. He left Lucy in the care

A remarkable story of love surviving for centuries has been told about Gatcombe Church.

of the court of Peter I of Cyprus and then joined that ruler's campaign in the Holy Land. Edward suffered a severe head wound during the campaign and returned to England brain damaged, unable to remember anything about the crusade. This was despite being given a splendid keepsake by Peter I, a sword with a chrysoberyl set in the hilt. The oak effigy on his tomb at one time held this sword.

Now the story moves forward five hundred years to the 1830s. A young woman from nearby Bowcombe finds herself drawn time and time again to Edward's tomb in Gatcombe church. She even dreams about Edward Estur. When the vicar of Gatcombe asks her why she spends so much time there she admits that she has fallen in love with the carved figure: 'I love to be with him and accompany him on his adventures in my thoughts and dreams,' she says.

Then one fateful day she makes her usual pilgrimage to Gatcombe. The weather is stormy and becomes worse while the girl is kneeling at the tomb of her hero. Soon a tempest is raging outside, accompanied by thunder and lightning, and to cap it all a total eclipse of the sun takes place. After the storm subsides and the darkness lifts, a passing farmer notices a horse, in a sweat of terror, tied up outside the church. He calms the animal and then enters the church. He finds it empty, but the effigy of Edward Ester is damaged. The chrysoberyl in the sword is missing. Despite extensive searches, neither the gem nor the young woman are seen again. The girl's name was Lucy Lightfoot.

This romantic yarn was in fact made up by the Reverend James Evans, who was rector at Gatcombe between 1965 and 1973. Despite its comparatively recent date, the story quickly became accepted as a genuine folk tale by later authors and some still believe it to be so.

SUPERSTITIONS

Before the second half of the 20th century, our rural ancestors were far closer to the land and much more aware of the changing seasons, nuances in the weather and the flora and fauna around them than the vast majority of us are today. However, this intimate knowledge was contrasted with a series of superstitions earnestly believed in without having any basis in fact.

There were a number of strange beliefs, for example, about the moon. It was considered unlucky to see the new moon through glass. It was always better to see it for the first time in the open air.

The waxing and waning of the moon was thought to affect not only the tides but the growth of all living things. In the days when blood-letting was commonly used by physicians to treat all sorts of ailments, it was believed that blood too had a tide affected by the moon. It was therefore thought best drained at the waxing of the moon to help draw out the badness believed to be in it. A child born under a waning moon would grow up to be less healthy, it was thought, than one born when the moon was waxing. Likewise, animals tended to be slaughtered when the moon was increasing, otherwise the meat might shrink when it was cooked.

The behaviour of birds and animals was taken to have special meaning, in superstitions perhaps dating back to our pagan past. At one time anglers believed that the behaviour of cattle reflected the likelihood or otherwise of catching fish. If the cattle were grazing, angling would be successful because the fish too would be feeding, but if they were lying down, the fish would be skulking away at the bottom of the streams, chewing the cud, so to speak.

We have already met with the tradition regarding St Swithun's Day (see the 'Kings and Saints' chapter). There are many other weather superstitions in old country lore. This is hardly surprising bearing in mind that the weather affected rural communities so significantly. Some of these beliefs pertained to wildlife. It was said, for example, that to hear a cuckoo stammer foretold coming rain, as did the screeching of a peacock. Rooks massing together while feeding and dogs eating grass were also thought to be an indicator of wet weather. Swallows flying high indicated warm, fine weather, but if they flew low it would be wet (no doubt this was truly indicated by the position in the atmosphere of the insects on which they were feeding). In regards to trees, it was also believed a wet spring was bound to follow if the leaves on the ash trees emerged before those of the oak. As a popular rhyme had it:

> If the ash is out before the oak,
> Look out, you'll get a soak.

In winter, if a cat was seen to turn her back on the fire and warm her behind, it was a warning that snow was on its way. A fire burning with a blue flame was also thought to indicate snow. A white hoar frost was supposed to warn of a coming storm. The whiter the frost, the more severe the storm. Some people called the sun's rays when they fell on rivers or ponds 'the sun's water pipes' and believed that the sun was replenishing its water pots with them. As soon as the pots were filled, it would pour them down as rain.

Almost everyone knows the old saw: 'Red sky at night, shepherd's delight; Red sky at morning, shepherd's warning.' Another rhyme gives the same virtue of predicting rain or shine to rainbows:

> Rainbow in the morning,

> Shepherds take warning;
> Rainbow afternoon,
> Good weather coming soon;
> Rainbow at night,
> Shepherd's delight.

It is difficult to know how a rainbow can be seen at night unless it's round the moon. Possibly the rhyme is referring to late summer's evenings. A more comprehensive, if even less likely, litany of rainbow superstitions can be found in the following rhyme:

> Rainbow in the south, heavy rain and snow;
> Rainbow in the west, little showers and dew;
> Rainbow in the east, fair skies and blue;
> Rainbow to windward, foul falls the day;
> Rainbow to leeward, damp runs away.

It was considered unlucky to point at a rainbow. One superstition stated that the arm used to point with would become paralysed as a result. There was a whole host of superstitions in which animals and birds were supposed to be lucky or unlucky. You will already be familiar with the rhyme about magpies: 'One for sorrow, two for joy etc.' It was said that if a crow crossed your path from left to right, this was a warning of coming misfortune, but if it crossed in the opposite direction, this was a good omen. A raven flying over a house or a robin flying into a house were both considered unlucky. The screech of a barn owl and a dog howling at night were both bad omens, as was a cock crowing at night, or laying an egg, or a hen laying unusually small eggs. Bees swarming on a Sunday also brought bad luck.

May blossom is one of the cheering sights of early summer but woe betide anyone who brought any into their home. *iStock*

Even pretty flowers could be looked on askance. It was a fairly universal belief that hawthorn (may) blossom would bring bad luck if it was brought into the house, and some said the same of snowdrops. Even the daffodil, that cheerful bloom which brightens many a home in early spring, had a bad reputation. It was forbidden in any household where chickens, ducks or geese were kept because it was believed the flowers would prevent them laying. Catkins would not only stop hens laying but any livestock giving birth until they were removed.

That so many superstitions pertained to bad luck rather than to good suggests our ancestors generally had a pessimistic outlook. It's a hint perhaps at just how uncertain and brief people's lives were in the past, before modern medicine existed or was freely available.

Our rural ancestors employed a whole range of folk remedies to try to cure themselves of any ailments that might afflict them. No doubt some of these, employing medicinal herbs, were genuinely efficacious, and an old belief that a spider's web wrapped round a cut would help it heal turned out to be true after penicillin was discovered: webs are often full of it. Many other remedies seemed logical but had no basis in modern medicine. Medieval herbalists believed in 'the doctrine of signatures', choosing herbs that vaguely resembled the parts of the body they hoped they'd treat. For example, lungwort, whose leaves resemble lungs, was presumed to be good for respiratory problems. Unfortunately, this optimistic approach rarely proved helpful.

Another commonly held belief was that a person's illness could be transferred to a living animal. For example, a ritual involved placing a live spider inside a walnut shell and then hanging this round the sick person's neck. As the spider died, it was thought, so would the illness. A popular method to remove warts involved rubbing the warts with a snail and then sticking the unfortunate creature on a hawthorn. As the snail rotted away, so would the warts. People seemed to be particularly bothered by warts in the past and there are numerous 'cures' on record to get rid of them. Another ritual involved laying a bag on a path containing the same number of grains of wheat or of pennies as the person had warts. Anyone foolish enough to pick up the bag would have the warts transferred to them.

Some folk remedies were even more bizarre. Moss found growing on a skull in a graveyard, if dried, ground and taken as snuff, was supposed to cure headaches. A fried mouse in breadcrumbs was given as a meal to children to cure them of wetting the bed. In the hope of taking away the dangerous disease of whooping cough, some people would clip off a lock of the hair of the afflicted child, make a sandwich of it and then feed it to a dog. There was no suggestion that the disease would be transferred to the animal, as in the examples above, but nevertheless this odd custom was believed to at least ease the cough. An even weirder remedy for whooping cough involved the catching of a trout (it had to be caught not bought), cooking it in cider and then cutting off the head. The head was placed inside the sick child's mouth, the fish's jaws outermost, and the child was then instructed to breathe through it!

In addition to these largely unaccountable remedies were charms, in the form of little prayers, that would be uttered by the sufferer or by those trying to help him. A charm for stopping the flow of blood, either after a wound or injury, or perhaps simply in the case of a nosebleed, went:

'In the name of the Father and of the Son and of the Holy Ghost
– Christ was born at Bethlehem – dipped in the river Jordan –
blessed that river and so it stood. So our Lord Jesus stop this blood.'

This approach was particularly popular for toothache. A typical
charm was:

'Peter sat at the gates of Jerusalem. Jesus Christ came by and said,
"What ailest thou?" "My teeth and bones do ache full sore." He
said, "Thy teeth and bones shall ache no more."'

In some versions Peter was replaced with the name of the sufferer.
The charm might also be written out on a piece of paper, folded
up and then worn round the neck until the toothache abated.
Clearly, these charms had little to do with orthodox Christian
theology but must have brought some comfort to the faithful.

Moss scraped from a skull found in a graveyard was one of the more grisly
ingredients used in folk medicine. *iStock*

THE JOURNEY THROUGH LIFE

Life was more precarious in the past. The lack of understanding as to what caused diseases or the knowledge of how to cure them meant mortality rates were high, especially among children. For the same reason, accidents involving injury were also far more serious. Wars were more frequent, too.

The perilous journey through life had important stages which were celebrated with ritual and accompanied by superstition. There were several strange beliefs regarding the beginning of life. It was said that a child born at midnight would have second sight and that a 'footling', that is one born feet first, would have magical powers. Efforts were made to preserve the caul surrounding the child at birth because it was thought to be possessed with sympathetic magic. Kept safe, it would prevent the person it belonged to ever suffering death by drowning. There are records well into the 20th century of sailors buying cauls in the belief they would keep them safe.

As soon as the mother entered labour, a party would be held at her house called a Merry Meet. The prospective husband would entertain family and neighbours and a 'groaning cheese' and a 'groaning cake' would be carefully cut into exactly the right number of pieces to serve to the guests. Unfortunately, of course, the woman giving birth was unable to enjoy the festivities herself.

With infant mortalities being so high, it was considered essential to christen the new-born baby as soon as possible. An unbaptised child would not go to heaven, but some thought they might become fairies instead. If the baptism was performed at home, the water used to christen the child was often thrown into the fire, to ensure it remained pure and that no evil influence could pollute it. While it was still unbaptised, it was customary to present the baby with an egg – symbolising new life – some salt and, unsafe though it may seem, a box of matches. Salt and fire were considered sure charms against the attentions of evil spirits.

Even after baptism, the infant might be under threat from fairies, who were thought to cast envious eyes at human children. To ward them off parents might hang over the crib a pair of scissors or tongs, which would dangle in the form of a cross. The cross-shape and the iron in the scissors were sure protection against the 'little people'. If fairies did get their hands on a baby, they would leave in its place a 'changeling', a peevish and ugly fairy child, or a block of wood so enchanted as to resemble the stolen infant. Babies who succumbed to what today we call cot-death were often thought to be the lifeless substitute left behind by kidnapping fairies.

An amusing superstition of the past saw some mothers biting their children's fingernails short rather than cutting them. They believed that if they cut the fingernails, the child would grow up to be a thief. It was also said that a new baby must always be carried upstairs before it goes down, otherwise it would not rise in life. If there were no stairs in the house, the midwife would climb onto a chair with it.

At one time new mothers genuinely feared their children might be stolen by fairies unless they protected them with certain charms before they were baptised.

At one time new mothers genuinely feared their children might be stolen by fairies unless they protected them with certain charms before they were baptised.

Moving on to young adulthood, there were also some interesting customs surrounding courtship. We tend to assume morals were more conservative in the past, so it may be a surprise to learn that courting couples were often allowed to sleep together undisturbed. However, this was only with the proviso that the young man kept his clothes on (minus his coat and boots). A variant custom called 'bundling' allowed the couple to share a bed with a bolster between them. Such would have been the disgrace if the young couple abused this trust that few did. Mind you, engagements tended to be shorter then.

A young woman hoping to marry into a farming family was often called upon to prove her strength by lifting with one arm the heavy lid of the parish chest in the church. The parish chest contained charitable donations and other valuables and was usually made of thick oak, bound with stout iron. To lift it with just one arm could be quite a feat.

As to the wedding day itself, there was an ancient custom in which the friends of the groom would call at the bride's house with the view of 'abducting' her. Her duty was to hide, so as to avoid this indignity, or better still to sneak to church before they caught her. This was a remnant of a custom known thousands of years ago in which young men would prove their worth by stealing the girl they fancied from under her parents' roof. In more civilised times, no abduction or manhandling of the bride actually took place and the whole thing was done in fun.

A rather unkind superstition relating to weddings was that if a woman served as a bridesmaid three times, she would never be married herself. Likewise, a man who acted as best man three times would never wed. But there are even stranger ones on record:

If a young woman puts on a man's hat or a young man puts on a woman's hat, they will have to wait three years before they can get married.

If a young person cuts bread obliquely or in uneven slices they will never be married, or will have to wait seven years, or they will end up with an objectionable mother-in-law.

If while sweeping a girl touches the foot of another girl with a broom she will rob that girl of her future husband.

When the bride enters the church, she must never look behind her or she will end up regretting the marriage.

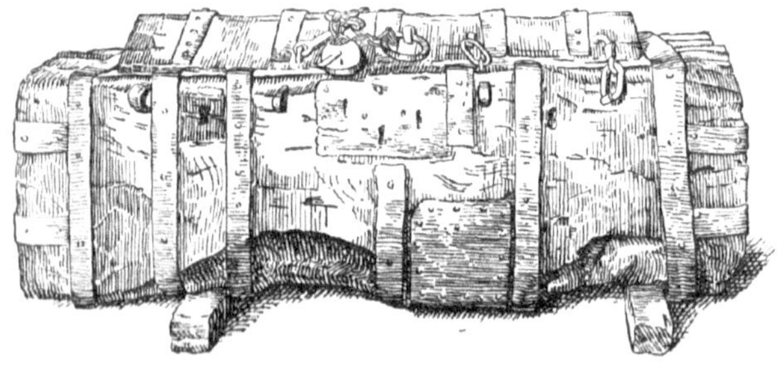

An example of a parish chest, an ancient and massive casket sometimes carved out of one solid piece of oak. Lifting its heavy lid with one arm would be hard work for most men, let alone the young women who were expected to do it.

There are equally strange superstitions regarding the really great change in a person's life – death. In the 'Superstitions' chapter several unlucky signs and portents were referred to, such as dogs howling and owls screeching, and these might equally be taken as omens of a coming death. There were many more. Clocks suddenly stopping or chiming thirteen were a bad sign, as were a robin tapping at the window pane, a crow getting into the house or an owl settling on the roof. Mysterious noises such as knocks and raps in the house where someone lay ill were also ominous. Carpenters sometimes claimed they heard sounds in their workshops at night resembling those of a coffin being made. They knew then that one would soon be ordered.

When the last moment had apparently come, people were sometimes 'helped to die' by those looking after them. All the doors and windows in the house were opened wide to allow the soul to escape. At the same time, knots were untied, mirrors covered and the fire – the 'soul of the house' – was put out. 'Passing bells' were traditionally rung nine times to announce a death but their original purpose was to scare away any evil spirits seeking to claim the soul of the departed. A plate of salt, that substance long believed to ward off evil, was placed on the body. No corpse was left with its eyes open for it was said that it would be looking for the next person to die.

After a death, the household would 'keep watch' for at least one night while the corpse lay in the house because it was thought that the soul of the departed might return. Sometimes the assembly would chant: 'It is for the last time, it is the last night', in order to remind the spirt that it had to pass on.

If the master of the house died, it was considered important to inform the bees in the hive of the fact, otherwise they'd all fly away. Any significant trees or bushes, even household plants, were at one time draped with black crepe after a death, otherwise it was feared they would wither away.

Once the corpse was conveyed to the burial place, it had to be taken to its grave in the same direction as the sun passes through the sky, that is 'deseal' or 'deosil'. To take it in the opposite direction, 'widdershins', would make the soul vulnerable to malign forces. There was a prejudice about being the first person buried in a new graveyard, because it was said that the Devil had the right to claim the first corpse. Another superstition had it that the spirit of the most recent person to be buried haunted the graveyard, watching over it until another burial took place.

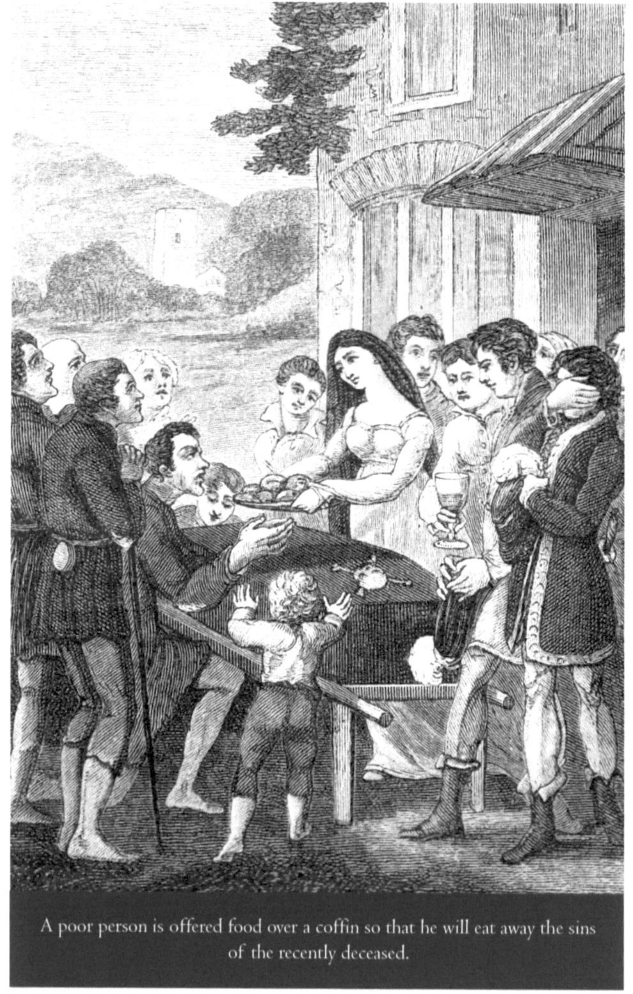

A poor person is offered food over a coffin so that he will eat away the sins of the recently deceased.

A decidedly primitive custom, which had all but died out by the end of the 19th century, was that of the 'sin-eater'. The sin-eater was usually a poor member of the parish who was prepared, for a small fee and a meal, to spiritually take on the sins of the person who had just died. This would be achieved by offering the man specially baked cakes, or bread on a dish of salt, the eating of which meant that he would absorb the sins. The food might even be offered over the coffin of the dead; at any rate it would always be eaten in the graveyard. This belief seems to hark back to the time when our most distant ancestors believed they could take on the power and attributes of a deceased person by devouring their body. The sin-eater was therefore a kind of spiritual cannibal.

THROUGH THE SEASONS

The rural calendar was marked by a series of high days and festivals intended to mark crucial times for sowing, reaping and other agricultural activities. These were often of great antiquity, pre-dating the Christian era. Many of them were adopted by the Church, although rededicated and renamed, and have therefore been preserved down the years.

The Celtic New Year was I November, when winter began. The coming dark days were defied with a great celebratory feast called Samhain. Bonfires were lit, animals were mated for the following spring and any surplus beasts were slaughtered to fatten everyone up in advance of the approaching cold. Guy Fawkes Night is a survival of the Samhain bonfire festival, merely put back a few days and given a political context which would have meant nothing to our pagan ancestors.

As a transient period, between the old year and the new, Samhain was considered a time when spirits from the underworld could revisit the earth. It was a time of ghosts and witches. This ancient belief is recalled in our still prevalent Halloween traditions. The Church diffused the apparent menace in this festival by dedicating I November to all the saints in heaven. 'Hallows' is an archaic word for 'saints', and Halloween is a contraction of 'All Hallows Eve', that is to say the night before All Hallows or All Saints Day. It was formerly the custom on I November to go Souling, roaming the parish in request of small gifts of money to be presented with specially baked dainties called soul cakes.

The next great festival in the Celtic calendar was Imbolc, on 1 February. This marked the beginning of the lambing season and is echoed in the Christian Feast of the Purification of the Virgin Mary, or Candlemas, celebrated the following day. Candlemas was dedicated to new mothers and childbirth.

The start of summer was celebrated on 1 May, in the Celtic festival called Beltane. Given over to fertility and the reawakening of the earth, this was a free-for-all party, with singing, dancing, the lighting of more bonfires and a certain amount of licence. May Day continued the tradition in a diluted form. Dancing round the maypole, a pretty ritual, probably replaced a more ribald ceremony.

The last of the big four Celtic festivals took place on August 1 and was called Lugnasad. This was the harvest festival, when the grain would be gathered in. The Christianised Saxons knew it as *hlaf-maesse*, meaning 'loaf-mass', which later became corrupted to Lammas or Lammastide. The first loaves of bread made from the gathered grain were dedicated to God in a more general Festival of the First Fruits.

In between these four seasonal festivals were many others, some of pagan and some of Christian origin, and others, like Easter and Christmas, a blend of the two. Lupercalia, the Roman celebration of youth, took place in the middle of February. In the warmer climes of the east it served as something of a harbinger of spring in which young people were encouraged to choose lovers. It had a reputation for excess, thoroughly defused by the adoption in its place of the feast honouring the martyrdom of St Valentine, which

The charming custom of dancing round the maypole had its origin in a pagan fertility festival. *iStock*

took place on 14 February. Valentine was a gentleman committed to chastity and it seems his association with romantic love was merely a matter of convenience. Nonetheless, St Valentine's Day remains one of the most popular traditions in the modern calendar, and people have been exchanging love tokens on this day for centuries.

Although Easter honours the Crucifixion and Resurrection of Christ, there are many secular traditions attached to it which date from pre-Christian times. Eggs are a natural symbol of rebirth and were equally appropriate for both the Resurrection and for spring, the season in which Easter falls. It was once a common pastime on Easter Day for people to roll gaily coloured hard-boiled eggs down hillsides in a jovial race. This was called 'pace-egging'. It has been suggested that the rolling eggs represented the life-giving sun's passage through the sky. It's likely that the name Easter has been borrowed from a pagan goddess of the spring, Eostre. The Easter Bunny may well be a descendant of the hare, an animal associated with the spring and fertility and sacred to the Celts.

'Lifting' was a widespread and peculiar custom carried out at Easter but which has now died out. It took place on Easter Monday and Tuesday. A chair would be garlanded with flowers and people would take it in turns to sit in it while their fellows raised them into the air. It was common for men to lift women on Monday and the other way round on Tuesday. A pleasant performance in the villages, it could be a rowdy affair in towns, where strangers were sometimes bundled into the chair and forced to pay a fee in order to be let down again. Folklorist Christina Hole has this to say about lifting:

'The usual explanation was that it was done in memory of our Lord's rising, but it is more probable that it was a survival of an old agricultural rite. In Central Europe girls leap through decorated hoops, saying "Grow flax, grow" as they do it, and the higher they leap the taller the flax will be. Lifting may have originated in something of the same kind.'

Hard-boiled 'pace eggs', brightly coloured with vegetable dyes, were rolled down hills in an old Easter custom. *iStock*

Other traditions relating to Easter are inarguably Christian, however. On Good Friday, the day of Christ's Crucifixion, we still eat Hot Cross Buns. At one time it was common for all loaves to be marked with a cross. Despite its name, Good Friday's association made it an unlucky one in the minds of our ancestors. It has become a bank holiday because those engaged in dangerous occupations, such as mining and fishing, refused to work on that day. Blacksmiths and those in the building trades would often down tools too because it was considered poor taste to handle nails on that day.

The following two days were quite different in character. Easter Sunday was always given over to worship and Monday was a holiday given over to leisure and sports. Some believed that the sun danced on Easter Day in joyous memory of the Resurrection and it was formerly a custom to rise before dawn in the hope of seeing this phenomenon. It was also traditional to wear new clothes on Easter Day, or at least one item that had never been worn before.

Beating the Bounds was another ritual commonly carried out at this time of the year, usually on Ascension Day (5 May). In the days before maps were freely available, it was important to clearly define parish boundaries and to ensure that nothing had occurred to alter them. Beating the Bounds was sometimes taken rather too literally, however. The villagers, accompanied by a clergyman, would take the young boys of the parish on a tour of the landmarks on its boundary. At each one they would pause and the boys would be whipped to make sure they remembered them. The clergyman would often bless the landmarks, too, especially wells.

The day before the feast of St John the Baptist is 23 June, or St John's Eve. It was also known as Midsummer Eve, even though the Summer Solstice – the longest day of the year – falls a couple of days before. Once again, this important stage in the year was celebrated with the lighting of bonfires.

There were numerous customs and celebrations associated with the bringing in of the harvest in the autumn. Fairs and sales were held at Michaelmas, on 29 September.

The strange custom of Lifting was popular on Easter Monday and the following Tuesday but has now completely died out.

The final great festival of the winter was, of course, Christmas. There is in fact no Biblical reference to the date of Christ's birthday and 25 December was chosen because it coincided with ancient pagan rituals associated with the Winter Solstice, the shortest day of the year, and with the birth dates of rival gods, such as Mithras: 25 December became the Festival of the Unconquered Sun during the reign of the Roman Emperor Aurelius. It made sense for the early Christians to adopt a day already given over to celebration, especially one relating to the sense of hope engendered by the start of longer days and shorter nights.

Many of the old, traditional customs associated with Christmas are of pre-Christian origin. Prince Albert, Queen Victoria's husband, is famously credited with bringing the custom of decorating a fir tree to Britain from his native Germany. In fact, there are records of an evergreen tree lit with candles being set up in a London street as long ago as the 15th century. This seems to have been a Norse tradition, as was the selecting of a Yule log, although the word 'Yule' has an Anglo-Saxon origin.

As we have seen, the lighting of fires was a central element of the ancient Celtic celebrations. Fire gave warmth and light, allowed food to be cooked and represented that great life-bringer, the sun. Fire therefore brought luck and scared away the powers of darkness. The Yule log would be selected with great ceremony and celebration, in much the way we would choose a Christmas tree today. The larger the fireplace, the larger the log chosen to fill it. Lighting the log became traditional on Christmas Eve and, if it was big enough, it might bring warmth throughout Christmas Day and beyond.

Holly became associated with Christmas because it is an evergreen, and mistletoe simply because it was the plant most sacred to our Celtic ancestors. According to a Roman historian, the Druids would only allow mistletoe to be cut with a golden sickle as it was so precious.

Cutting and bringing home the Yule log was a major occasion in big houses during the run-up to Christmas. *iStock*

The Twelve Days of Christmas, which included our present New Year's Day and Twelfth Night (6 January), were the perfect excuse for having a good time. Where possible, big family gatherings would be held, or feasts where the servants as well as the masters would be entertained. Carols would be sung by the poor, and extra pennies collected to help them celebrate later on. A more boisterous variant on carol singing was the traditional wassailing. Wassail is an Old English word meaning 'be of good cheer'. Poor people would walk round the parish singing wassailing songs either for money or, more usually, for beer. Those better off might have in their possession a wassail cup, large and often of elaborate design, which they would fill with mulled beer or wine and use it to toast each other. Mummers Plays – medieval morality plays – were also performed in many places.

In a custom dating back to Roman times, the roles of master and servant were overturned on one day of the year around Christmas time, with the staff served a feast by their employers. Sometimes a Lord of Misrule might be appointed from among the servants, a kind of fool king. In some military regiments today the officers serve Christmas dinner to their men. A charming custom was to lay the table for two on Christmas Eve to 'welcome Joseph and Mary on Christmas morning'. There was also a superstition that animals were able to talk on Christmas morning and some people, particularly children, would creep to the pens and cowsheds as the sun rose in the hope of catching them doing so.

Finally, it was also traditional to celebrate New Year's Day with a party, reflecting the universal belief that it is lucky to begin anything in good spirits. Of course, this tradition still holds true today.

Mistletoe, an unusual plant that is a parasite on other trees, is now closely associated with Christmas but at one time it was venerated by the Druids.
iStock

More Legends & Folklore books from Bradwell Books for you to enjoy.

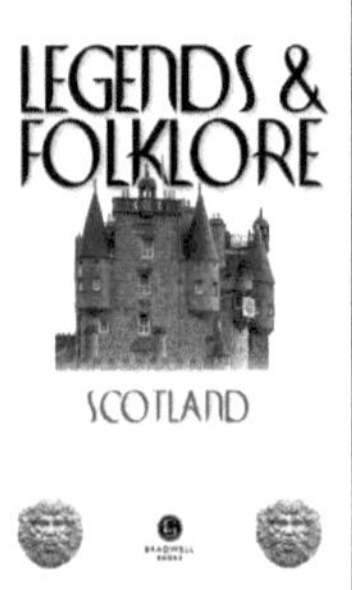

Visit www.bradwellbooks.co.uk for more details